T5-AWA-993

Silence of the Tongue

*What happens when a pastor is diagnosed
with tongue cancer?
A Testimony of Words and Unity*

ERIC G. ZEIDLER

All rights reserved. No part of this publication may be reproduced, stored in a retrieval system, or transmitted in any form or by any means—electronic, mechanical, photocopy, recording, or any other—except for brief quotation in printed reviews, without the prior permission of the author or where applicable the publisher.

ISBN: 978-0-9889866-4-0 (paperback)
ISBN: 978-0-9889866-5-7 (ebook)

Copyright © 2014 by Eric Zeidler
Published by: The Glory Cloud publications LLC
PO Box 193, Sicklerville NJ 08081
theglorycloudpublications.com
Cover Design & Typesetting—TGC publications
Cover Photography — Eric Zeidler

I want to thank my family Deziree, Richelle, Chocky (my mom), Nan—my mother-in-law, and many relatives who were there for me, and especially my wife, Jaimie, who has been there for 34 years, through the operation, and continues to be my uplifting support.

Additionally, I thank Doug and Joanne Johnston for allowing me to complete this book in a peaceful place. I also want to thank the many pastors, leaders, and The River Church members, who were there, when I could not be. I express much gratitude to the Hospital of the University of Pennsylvania for their incredible support through their nurses and doctors. And thanks to, Min. Terrence Clark for encouraging me and working with me on this project.

And thanking the most important person, I thank my Lord and Savior Jesus Christ, for walking with me through the storm. The Holy Spirit for guiding me in this book and my Father GOD for allowing me to go through this—to share with the Body of Christ your love, unity, and compassion.

"Eric is a great pastor, friend, and a true blessing to me and my family. What an inspiration Pastor Eric is! His love is evident, and best shown through his kindness, and compassion for the needy and homeless.

When he was battling cancer of the tongue, in the natural it looked like he would lose the battle and even lose his life. Or, if he did live, he would never be able to speak, or preach again. But thanks be to God; he is alive and preaching with more anointing and power than ev-er."

—Pastor Joe Panzino —
God is the Answer Ministries

"I count Eric as one of my best friends and coworkers for Christ. We have never discussed our differences and always are able to celebrate our oneness in Christ"

—Pastor Dave Repenning—
Elmer United Methodist Church

"Pastor Eric is a man who exemplifies the compassion of Christ. His commitment to the integrity of the Word of God, his congregation, and the lost in his community and cities beyond is second to none. His innovative vision extends beyond the church walls, and his empathy knows no bounds. Glad to have worked alongside this true brother in the Lord!"

—Big Bass Bill—
WXGN Ocean City, NJ

"I've known Pastor Eric only a few years, although it seems like many more. He has joined my circle of faith-filled friends who I can truly enjoy sincere fellowship in the Spirit.

I share with him the triumph over cancer (1998). His testimony and book share the physical, emotional and spiritual trials that even faith filled people have experi-enced and overcome.

It was an honor when he asked my company to publish his first book. May it reach the multitudes around the world."

—Rev. Terrence Clark —
Founder of The Glory Cloud publications LLC

"If all my talents and powers were to be taken from me by some inscrutable providence, and I had my choice of keeping but one, I would unhesitatingly ask to be allowed to keep the power of speaking, for through it, I would quickly recover all the rest"

—Daniel Webster

TABLE OF CONTENTS

CHAPTER ONE
THE DAY IT HAPPENED

Who could ever imagine a preacher losing his tongue, or not being able to communicate without using speech? As hard as that is to imagine, in August of 2006, this pastor was faced with a dilemma that could have taken that direction.

Proverbs 18:21 *Death and Life are in the power of the tongue, and they that love it shall eat the fruit thereof."*

This scripture became the passage that I stood on in prayer, and the Lord explained this scripture, along with 1 Cor. 12: 12-26, to me as I started down the road to cancer recovery.

All my life it seems my teeth have been my downfall. I think I have enough fillings in my mouth to fill the Grand Canyon. One day in 2006 while I was eating, I felt a hard piece of something as I started to bite down. Oops! A piece of filling came out. As with most men, I do not like to admit when I have a problem. We think it will just go away. So, I waited for about two weeks expecting something to happen—and it did. It started to get a little painful. My lovely wife, with a tremendous amount of wisdom, said to me, "Why don't you make an appointment with the dentist and see what is the problem?"

By now, I needed to go. Yes, it was a filling. After the dentist had filled the tooth, the pain seemed still to be there. Soon, I noticed there was a sore starting to form on the side of my tongue that looked pretty strange. Again, I just passed it off thinking I must have bit my tongue while eating. After a few more days, the pain seemed to get worse, and the sore seemed to be getting bigger. Now, I didn't want to hear that voice again say, "Why don't you make an appointment with the dentist?" So, I called and had him take a look at it.

Dr. Nester was a little concerned. He gave me some ointment to put on it and said to come back again in a week. The pain persisted, the sore got bigger, and difficulty with eating had increased. Going back for the follow-up changed the direction of my life forever. He took one look at the tongue, and the sore, and was concerned about the pain that seemed to persist, and recommended I go see an oral surgeon immediately. This is when I noticed God was starting to show Himself, in the direction, and pathway ahead.

No matter how we feel, or what is going on in our life, rest assured that God knows.

Romans 8:28 *And we know that all things work together for good to them that love God, to them who are the called according to his purpose.*

My dentist contacted the local oral surgeon, it was about 3:50 pm and the office closed at 4:00 pm. However, the doctor said, "Send him over immediately, and I will see him."

Just a short drive later, I arrived at the oral surgeon's office with no idea what was about to happen. As a pastor, there are times God raises you up to be prepared for events that are about to happen. It's called "Grace."

2 Cor. 12:9 *And he said unto me, My grace is sufficient for thee, for my strength is made perfect in weakness.*

The oral surgeon took one look in my mouth and said, "You have a tumor growing on the side of your tongue."

This was on a Friday, and the doctor had no office hours until Monday, but he walked me into the nurse's office and said, "I need to see him tomorrow for a biopsy."

The nurse said, "You are not scheduled in the office for tomorrow."

The doctor replied, "For him, I will come in."

Thank God for His favor, and His hands being upon this situation.

The very next day, Saturday morning, I was in his office. The doctor started by numbing my tongue and cutting off a small part of the inflamed area to be biopsied. Now, it was waiting time till Monday, to learn the results.

Now, you may think, it was the time for anxiety to set in, and I would be a basket case. But, I was already focused on that Sunday's message, and sharing the Word to the congregation at The River Church. There was a peace that came upon me, for I had to believe that God knew exactly what was about to happen.

That Monday morning, I received a phone call from the doctor's office asking Jaimie and me to come to his office for a consultation on the results of the biopsy. I knew in my heart that something was serious.

At his office, the doctor sat us down and said, "Eric, the biopsy came back positive for cancer."

What would be your response?

Many people say that when they hear about the BIG C, they get scared, fear sets in, and tears start to run. Thank God He was already preparing us for the next step. The peace that only Jesus can give came over us.

John 14:27 *Peace I leave you, my peace I give you; not as the world giveth, give I unto you, Let not your heart be troubled, neither let it be afraid.*

The next step was all God.

The doctor recommended I see the number one oral surgeon at the University of Pennsylvania Hospital. Without any hesitation, my wife and I called him as soon as we arrived home. The receptionist asked, "Can you come in tomorrow?"

Now that's God's favor. The most important step in this whole process was how quickly everything moved.

As a pastor, many people come to me dealing with sickness, disease, financial issues, marital problems, and much more. The very thing that I ask all of them, "Is there something in your life right now that is wrong, or hindering God from moving in your life?"

For example there are only two causes for sickness:

1. STUPIDITY- we can't blame God or the devil. We go out into the cold and work with no coat on. We eat things we know are not good for us. When we get sick, because our body reacts negatively to perverse environment or poor nutrition, we want to blame something or somebody. We do not want to take any responsibility for our own actions.

2. SIN - Sometimes it's because of the sin in our lives or the sin in the world.

James 5:13, 14 *Is any among you afflicted? Let him pray. Is any merry? Let him sing psalms. Is any sick among you? Let him call for the elders of the church; and let them pray over him, anointing him with oil in the name of the Lord. And the prayer of faith shall save the sick and the Lord shall raise him up; and if he has committed sins, they shall be forgiven him. Confess your faults one to another, and pray one for another, that ye may be healed.*

Notice in the scriptures how sickness and sin are connected? Respectively, sickness is also caused from unforgiveness or bitterness.

Ephesians 4:31-32 *Let all bitterness and wrath and anger and clamor and slander be put away from you, along with all malice. And be kind to one another, ten-derhearted, forgiving each other, just as God in Christ Jesus also has forgiven you.*

So, what does a pastor do when faced with the same diagnosis? I searched my heart!

That night, when Jaimie and I got home from the doctor's office, after receiving this news of cancer, I did what the Word of God says. I told Jaimie that I would be in our bedroom praying and I did not want to be disturbed. I had to get on my knees, and ask the Lord to seek and search my heart. I had to see if I had offended anyone, caused any strife or bitterness, or spoken about anyone in a way that would harm my walk with Him.

After an hour or so, the Holy Spirit brought to my mind a few things that I had to clear up. I made a few phone calls, and repented and asked for forgiveness from a few people. Then I asked the Lord, "Do you want me to proceed with the visit to the doctor's office at the University of Penn, or wait on you for healing?"

You see, I also believe, God can heal cancer and can heal diseases. I have seen miracles. I have seen God change hearts that could never be changed by anyone else. I felt peace that God wanted to use this as a testimony in my life. So, I told the Lord, "I will go. Use me and show me what you need me to do."

The question many ask is "Why Me?" But, I said, "Why not me, Lord?"

CHAPTER TWO
PREPARE FOR HEALING

How do you prepare yourself for something you know nothing about? We all can choose to surrender to man's thinking, or research the Word of God for answers. Many times, it has been said, the "B-I-B-L-E" stands for Basic Instructions Before Leaving Earth. I take that literally.

The Bible (God's Word) is the truth, and in it, you can find everything you need to survive and get through daily life. As my journey started, I arrived at the University of Penn for a consultation with Dr. O'Malley, the head of the Otorhinolaryngology Department. (Yes, say that three times fast.)

Jaimie and I had a long conversation with the two doctors that would be doing the surgery. They were Dr. O'Malley and Dr. Chalian. Dr. O'Malley would do the main surgery of performing a tracheotomy and removing the tumor and Dr. Chalian would do the reconstructive surgery. The doctors shared the positive and negative of the surgery, explaining the operation would take up-wards to 18 hours, and that recovery would be about 4 months.

Since I would have a tracheotomy in my throat to help me breath, talking would be out for a while, and of course preaching would be on hold. With that in mind, I needed to prepare and get things in order, at home, at church, and in my life.

One of my close friends, Pastor Joe Panzino, who himself battled death through a strange disease that tried to kill him many years earlier, explained to me about juicing. These liquefied vegetables, fruits, and nuts would start the healing process in my blood stream before the operation.

Excited about taking his counsel, I decided to take that wisdom and seek the Lord on instructions. The Lord took me to Daniel 1:8-17—

Vs.8 *But Daniel purposed in his heart that he would not defile himself with the portion of the king's meat, not with the wine which he drank, therefore he requested of the prince of the eunuchs that he might not defile himself.*

Vs. 12 *Prove thy servants I beseech thee, ten days; and let them give us pulse to eat, and water to drink.*

Pulse is the fiber of fruit, vegetables, and nuts. I would blend these together into a drink and have that instead of eating food. Ten days prior to the operation, I started a daily diet of fruit, vegetables, and water. My body even started to feel stronger and many things started to fall into place.

Remember, when God gives you a Word, you can trust Him, and believe, He has the best for you. During the ten days that I was on the regimen of pulse and water, something incredible happened, confirming God's Word, in Daniel 1:8-17, was working according to His plan.

I was working on something around the house, when I noticed blood on my finger. When I looked down, I saw a large open cut. I immediately went to clean and bandage it. It didn't need stitches, but it was a deep cut. I thought about the operation and others that I knew who had major operations. I remembered, sometimes surgeons put off surgery, if there is an exposed cut. Doctors do not want any accidental infections to happen during surgery.

So, I made sure it was properly cleaned. After about three to four days, I took off the bandage, and I noticed that the cut was healed. The slice that looked deep was hardly seen, and there was very little trace of any cut at all. I was so happy. Not only because the cut had healed, but I knew then, God had prepared my body for the surgery scheduled in a few days.

Are you starting to see, how God can take anything, and turn it around for something good?

Excitement for the surgery, and what God was going to do, now radiated in my heart. It was an excitement that I cannot explain. Jaimie and I were about to go on a ride that would take us into the unknown.

Stop and think, if God were to speak to you and say, "If you do this you won't die."

How many would listen and do what He asked? I believe, probably all of us. Yet, we have no idea that the foods we eat, the liquid we drink, and even the air we breathe, can destroy our lives.

I recalled a true story. A certain man, who went into a certain laboratory, inquired the lab researcher about a popular snack cake, he noticed in the lab, on a glass dish, under a glass dome. The researcher explained that the spongy treat had been there for fifteen years, as part of an experiment. The observation revealed that over that time, there weren't any bugs or bacterial growth on it.

There are foods that we eat that are nothing more than chemicals and fake sugar to make our taste buds want more. Our blood stream is remarkable. It regenerates each night and cleanses itself. Think about when we get up in the morning. We grab a cup of coffee and a donut, and then we run to work.

This is an example of a fire in a fireplace. During the night, the fire starts to go out, and in the morning there are embers of hot fire left. If we put big green logs, that have not been seasoned, into the fire, it would smother and most likely go out. But, if we load the fireplace with kindling wood and fan the flame, before you know it, we have a blazing fire going. And, whatever you throw into the fire at that time, will burn.

Our bodies are just like this example. When we get up, and it's tough to get going, we load our bodies with sugar, sweets, etc... It seems to give us energy. But after a while, we get sluggish, tired and lazy. The reason, because we, like the fire, put on green unseasoned logs and the energy went out.

But, if we feed our bodies with vegetables, fruits, nuts, and grains, our bodies will start a fire burning again. Before you know it, its lunch time, and we load it again, to burn all day.

I understand that my blood stream is the life blood to my body for healing. What I put in my body, helps me to fight off bacteria and disease. Don't let your blood stream be like a cesspool. God has provided all the foods we need to sustain a long life.

Psalms 139:14 *I will praise thee; for I am fearfully and wonderfully made;*

Now I am ready.

"God, only you know, and only you can guide and lead us now. "

What a day it was to walk into the hospital with an excellent attitude, skipping and singing, my body prepared for healing. Only God knew what lay ahead and what the outcome would be. You see, I told the congregation that if for some reason, I lost my tongue, and I was no longer able to speak, I would learn sign language and shout at them with my fingers!

God had placed a calling on my life to preach the living Word of God and "no weapon formed against me shall prosper."

Now, before I tell you about this operation, I have to mention someone who is my support, my rock, my better half; my wife Jaimie. I cannot even imagine what was going through her mind at this point while she waited out in the waiting room. Although my daughters, Deziree and Richelle along with others of my family were there with her, what was going through her mind? We had talked about this day many nights prior to the operation. We both had peace about whatever would happen.

My heart was right and ready. We trusted in the Lord for His sovereign will to be done. The dominating reason for our peace was that I would win either way. If I died on the operating table for some reason, I was going home to be with my first love— Jesus. If the operation was a success, then I would also win.

I grabbed a hold of Jaimie's hand and we did what we know is true; we prayed and asked the Lord for strength, peace, and joy, and healing. When it was time to go back to the preparation room, we kissed, and looked at each other in a way that only we knew in our hearts. Sometimes words cannot express what the eyes reveal.

As they were wheeling me back to prep, I could only do one thing—SING, SING, and Praise Him. The people all around me must of thought that I was a crazy man, but I was about to go on a ride and Jesus had the wheel.

Sixteen hours later, the surgery was complete. I was wheeled back into the ICU room and I can only imagine what my family saw. Tubes were everywhere, blood was everywhere, and monitors were beeping, and nurses were tending to my needs. Both of my daughters came in, while I was still out from the anesthesia. They had to leave the room due to the stress of seeing their father lying in the bed hooked up to all of this. They admitted that they were not prepared to experience what they saw. But Jaimie, my rock, was there and never left my side.

Throughout these chapters you will see and experience God's miracle-working power. From the beginning to today, He has never left me nor abandoned me.

And now for another miracle, when I awoke from the operation, the nurses gave me instructions to help ease pain. They showed me how to buzz them for help in case of an emergency. They explained to me, there were two button controls on my chest. One to contact them for anything I needed and the other was a morphine button for pain. The morphine button would send the drug through my IV line, every fifteen minutes as needed. All this way, I had trusted that God had a plan, and I believed a miracle was possible.

God has a funny way of getting people's attention at times. The nurses were my second line of evangelism. Yes, whenever the nurses came in they would ask me, "Mr. Zeidler, why are you not using your morphine button?"

I would reply, "Because I have no pain."

A miracle! If you would have seen what I looked like, you would have most likely pushed the button for me at times. Oh, by the way, my reply was never with my voice, because of the tracheotomy. Writing on a tablet for the next few weeks was my mode of communication.

For three days and nights the nurses could not figure out why I did not need any pain killers. I know they were giving me medication, but as for the morphine button, it was never used.

The doctors were so impressed with my healing rate; they decided to take me to a regular room where I would recover. I remembered what God told me ten days earlier about Daniel. I was seeing first-hand how the scriptures and God's wisdom works. God had prepared my body for healing and His hands were all over the plan.

My best man Dominic and his family had provided a blessing that was awesome. They had some influence to get me into a private room. What a blessing and what dear friends. There I am in a private room. The doctors are very pleased with the fast recovery. God is in control. Things are going real well. You know when it seems things are going great, how the enemy raises his ugly head. Accordingly, I was about to experience another turn.

CHAPTER THREE
GIVE ME A MINISTRY, LORD

So what did the doctors do? Throughout those sixteen hours, while I was on the operating table, the doctors and nurses were very busy. Dr. O'Malley, the chief surgeon, installed a tracheotomy into my throat, and prepared me for a long surgery. This operation is called a flap. The process was to cut from under my left ear, down below the throat, across to the right side, stopping about one inch below the other ear.

They had to remove the tumor from my left side of the tongue, which had grown to the size of a quarter, and about a quarter inch thick. They pulled the skin from under my chin and lay it over my face so they can get at the tongue. Later, they told me that this operation is so that they can remove the tongue through the jaw, to get access to the place of surgery. Still being done today, this method, assisted by the use of a computer robotic arm, has made the operation shorter and easier for the doctors.

15

After removing the tumor, they cut and removed a large piece of my left arm with the major vein that gives it blood. Dr. Chalian now had the painstaking task to attach my arm segment to the right side of my tongue. Amazing how doctors with the hand of God can recreate a tongue so I can speak.

Oh, by the way, as they were cutting the tongue, they stopped about a half centimeter short, (and I know God's hands was there) so that I would be able to speak. The next task was to remove a patch of skin from my left leg and graft it to my left arm, to repair the area that was used to reconstruct my mouth. This part of the surgery was told to me after the operation, by both doctors. My greatest thanks go to them for an amazing operation, with the assistance of God Almighty.

In chapter 2, I explained I was about to experience another attack from the enemy. Here is how it went. Every day and night the nurses would come in and take my vital signs. They had a small device called a Doppler that was the size of a pen. They would take this Doppler and place it on the reconstructed side in my mouth. They would listen to the blood rushing in and out, so they could be sure it was flowing properly.

It had only been one day. I was in a regular room. It was Sunday morning. Jaimie and the leaders of the church were preparing for a wonderful day. I was resting comfortably as the healing process continued. At about 6:30 a.m., in the early morning, the nurse came in my room for the standard vital signs and Doppler check. As she came in her face had a look of concern—no, urgency! She came closer to the side of my bed and looked at my mouth. At this time, I started to feel something different in my mouth, like my tongue was getting bigger, or something was happening. She called on the phone for the resident doctor to come into the room STAT. When you hear the word STAT, it makes you wonder what is going on at the moment.

The resident doctor came in within a minute or two, picked up the phone, and said prepare the emergency room, for an emergency operation. What had happened? During the night, I had received a blood clot in the left side of my mouth, my arm-side. Blood was flowing into my arm-side of my tongue, but was not flowing out. Within ten minutes, I was now waiting in the operating room for another surgery.

When the nurse came in and said there was a problem, again, as a pastor, I remembered—the first thing I did was close my eyes and prayed to take authority over the situation in Jesus' name.

Ephesians 6:12 *For we wrestle not against flesh and blood, but against principalities, against powers, against rulers of the darkness of this world, against spiritual wickedness in high places.*

What did this all mean? It meant I was under attack again, but "greater is He that is within me, than he that is in this world."

I prayed in the name of Jesus, the one who had been with me the whole time and had guided me. I knew that He had a greater purpose for me. As I share later in this book, our WORDS are very powerful, sharper than any two-edged sword, and able to fight that which is unseen.

After the operation, which took three hours, they transferred me back to my private room for comfort and healing. As I rested, a thought came to me, and I prayed, "Lord, give me a ministry here at the hospital while I am healing."

Always be careful of what you ask, because God sees your heart. And despite the place where we are, and the surroundings you are in, He will answer you.

Jeremiah 33:3 *Call unto me, and I will answer thee, and show thee great and mighty things, which thou knowest not.*

As I called on Jesus, to show me what was next, He reminded me that sometimes in our life, pain and suffering is part of the process of life. Jesus didn't ask to go to the cross, but it was part of God's plan of redemption for us. Jesus didn't ask for the pain and suffering, but it was part of the process to gain victory.

The days went by, and the healing was getting faster. The vital signs were better, and things were looking good. It was time to get up and start walking. If you have been in the hospital for any length of time, you know that the start of getting up is always a treat. Now remember, I asked the Lord for a ministry. I was starting to walk with my IV pole and the ministry I asked for was starting to become clear. At first, I could only walk for a short period, but as days went by, I began feeling very comfortable walking by myself.

I had to walk four times a day. One day, early in the morning, as I started to walk, I realized that I was on the cancer patient floor. Everyone there had cancer or was a cancer patient. Walking down the hall, I started going into rooms. Because I could not speak, I started to smile and wave. At that moment, because I had not yet looked at myself, I had no idea how my smile looked. I didn't know if it was so ugly that I shouldn't be doing this.

All my life people have told me, no matter where you go, you always have a smile on your face. What better ministry for me than to encourage people with a smile. As I walked, smiled and waved, it became clear. The ministry God gave me was to encourage others who were feeling down, depressed, and unloved. While I did this, I felt so much better seeing the smiles of those new friends of mine. Hours went by, the walks began to strengthen me, and bring hope to those who were battling this terrible disease.

I remember one day, when I was feeling a little down, due to lack of sleep, I missed a few walks. Lying there, looking out at the helicopter pad, through the window, and watching the helicopters come in with emergency patients, I realized God gave me another ministry—Intercession. I said to myself, "While I am here, whenever someone comes in or goes out by helicopter, it is an opportunity for me to pray—speak healing and comfort to all the people I don't know—flying to or from the hospital."

1Timothy 2:8 *I will therefore that men pray every-where, lifting up holy hands, without wrath and doubt-ing.*

One afternoon, the nurse came into my room after resting and asked me, "Did you walk yet today?"

I replied, "Not yet."

The nurse replied, "The patients on the floor are waiting for you."

Then it hit me, I am a pastor and now my flock is here on my hospital floor. I had a new mission and calling while I was hospitalized. It was to get up, and go visit my congregation. My new mission was starting to excite me more and more. There was one member of my hospital congregation, a man who had a tumor on the side of his head that made him look like the Elephant Man. My heart broke every time I stopped to see him. I would walk in and smile and wave. He did all the talking. (It's amazing how you learn to listen when you can't speak.) I would hold his hand. With my hands, I explain to him, I was praying for him daily. He would smile and then I would continue to do my rounds to the other patient congregants.

I have a special place in my heart for being at the right place, at the right time, to be God's hands extended. We sometimes take life for granted. Life is to be lived, not for ourselves, but for others. There is more pleasure in giving than receiving.

Then there were those times that you have to laugh, like when friends from church, Skip and Judy, came to see me one afternoon. I had a mask on that would mist wet air, so my throat would not dry out. As they walked in, they saw me connected to tubes and blood bags—hanging from my neck for drainage. Judy's eyes said it all. She didn't know what to think of what was lying in the bed.

Conversation was limited due to not being able to speak. So, I wrote on my writing pad and asked if they would like to walk down the hall. They agreed. As I looked at Skip and Jaimie, I winked. They knew I was up to something. As Judy was watching every move I made, I took off the mist mask and started to gasp for air, as if my oxygen was being depleted. Her eyes almost popped out. She went into emergency mode. Then, she remembered, it wasn't oxygen, but a mist mask. We all laughed; enjoying the joy we have and share with each other, and the Lord.

I remembered a day when I was feeling down, looking out at the helicopter pad, and asking the Lord a question.

"Lord" I said, I don't smoke. I don't drink. No one in my family has ever had cancer. Others who have abused their bodies and have never had cancer seem to get away without this kind of pain. I really don't deserve this Lord."

Then a small still quiet voice responded in my heart, "Neither did my Son deserve it either, but like you, He was willing to do that which was needed to help others."

As you may understand, I began to weep and cry as I understood exactly how selfish that question was. If we are open to God's answers, we can learn so much. It is at times like these that He ministers to our hearts.

Later on that day the man with the cancerous tumor on the side of his head came into my room. There were about six family members with him. He was in a wheel chair. He was being released from the hospital early. When he came in, he smiled and thanked me for being a friend, and an encouragement to him, while he was in the hospital. He said, "May the Spirit of the Lord be upon you," and he and his family left.

Yep, I started to weep again, as it moved my heart.

There was a team of doctors and interns that would come into my room every day. They checked on my status, my healing, and my arm-tongue. They would always come at the end of their rounds. Each day, when they came in, they would always say, "Hi, how are you feeling today?"

I would smile, nod, and write my answer on my pad. This day they said, "We want to thank you for going around and being a blessing to others on this floor. "

Yep, I started to weep.

God was speaking to me in many different ways, through people, to help me understand that He had a plan. Then they said, "The reason we come into your room last, is because after a long day, your smile, and pleasant attitude, helps us realize it is all worth it."

Yep, weeping again.

How can one explain, how God uses people in many different situations—to minister, encourage, build up, and just be there for others? My whole life, in the ministry, has always been for the Body of Christ. Different backgrounds, origins of people, races, and different forms of worship, bring us all together, to see God's plan through His Son Jesus. And yet, God was about to take me to another level, in the hospital, to explain and encourage me about the Body of Christ.

Several years prior to this operation, I was praying and worshiping the Lord one night. In the still of the evening, the Lord showed me a vision of the Body of Christ. I saw two outstretched arms, in front of me, of Jesus's hands. I knew they were His, because there were two piercings in the wrist of each arm. In one hand, there was a straight edge razor. He was taking it and cutting the wrist of His other arm. He said to me, "This is what the Body of Christ is doing to itself."

As I stood there and wept, I realized, not just what I do when I irreverently talk about someone else, criticize someone else, or reject someone else, but what all Christians do to each other as the Body of Christ. I think my words are making me feel better, but in actuality, I'm hurting HIS body. Jesus is the head and we are His body. Whenever, we do something to someone else, we hurt HIM.

CHAPTER FOUR
WHAT IS IN MY MOUTH?

1 Cor. 12:12-26 *For as the body is one, and hath many members, and all the members of that one body, being many, are one body; so also is Christ. For by one Spirit are we all baptized into one body, whether we be Jews or Gentiles, whether we be bond or free; and have been all made to drink into one Spirit.*

For the body is not one member, but many. If the foot shall say, Because I am not the hand, I am not of the body; is it therefore not of the body? And if the ear shall say, Because I am not the eye, I am not of the body; is it therefore not of the body? If the whole body were an eye, where was the hearing? If the whole were hearing, where was the smelling? But now hath God set the members, every one of them in a body, as it hath pleased him. And if they were all one member, where were the body? But now are they members, yet but one body. And the eye cannot say unto the hand, I have no need of thee; not again the head to the feet, I have no need of you. Nay, much more those members of the body, which seem to be more feeble, are necessary: And those members of the body, which we think to be less honourable, upon these we bestow more abundant honour; and our uncomely parts have more abundant comeliness. But our comely parts have no need; but God hath tempered the body together, and having given more abundant hounor to that part which lacked. That there should be no schism in the body, but that the member should have the same care one for another. And whether one member suffer, all the members suffer with it; or one member be hounored, all members rejoice with it.

I had been in the hospital now for about seven days. God had been doing some amazing things. People were being touched. Concertedly, God was applying that same grace, faith, and understanding to my heart.

God can use many different things to get your attention. Assuredly, the greatest way is the Word of God. He reveals Himself, in ways that He desires, to get your undivided attention, this happened to me several nights around 3:30 a.m. in the morning.

One particular night, would be a special night that would change my life—again, forever. It was a night, just like any other. The nights before, when it seemed like Jesus had walked into my room, I could sense love and cozy comfort. Unexpectedly, this night was to be something special.

I was sitting wide awake, with my thoughts in prayer. That still small voice that speaks to you in the quiet of the moment said, "What do you have in your mouth?"

I can only imagine what that voice was like when God called Moses from out of the burning bush, or Abraham to leave his family and go to a place that God would send him, or other great men and women of the Bible. Those who have heard that small still voice and came to attention. It is the response of a soldier, to his commander who suddenly walked into the room. It's like being in the middle of the room, when your wife starts to talk. You can hear her from the other side of the room because you love, and recognize her voice.

John 10:4 *And when he putteth forth his own sheep, he goeth before them, and the sheep follow him; for they know his voice.*

The voice was very clear, and I heard it in my spirit. I responded. "Lord what do you mean? What do I have in my mouth?"

I wasn't eating anything. I had no other objects in my mouth. I heard, "What do you have in your mouth?" Again, I replied. "Lord, I do not know what you are try-ing to say to me."

Sometimes, it is good to ask the Lord a question, as if you are a three-year-old. The Lord then responded with clarity. "What you have in your mouth is the Body of Christ?"

Still, I was more puzzled then before, because I was having a conversation about something God knew, but I was trying to figure out. One of the awesome things about God, He will tell you over and over until you get it. You know, "Hello—is anyone there?"

Then the most profound statement from His Word came to me. 1 Corinthians 12:12-26 about the Body of Christ. He said to me, "What you have in your mouth is the Body of Christ. Your arm, a lessor member of your body that does nothing, which has no taste buds, and should not be in your mouth, has now become a very important part of your mouth, for you to use to speak. Your tongue accepted your arm, a more important member, and they have been sown together as one, they now can produce something that is so wonderful and positive. "

Who would have ever thought that a piece of meat on your arm could ever become a tongue? As I sat there weeping and meditating on what the Lord just told me, I was still in a state of quiet, peaceful, wondering. What was God up to?

The very next day was the first day I had an opportunity to see my face and my mouth. I didn't realize that there was a mirror under the eating table that was in front of me. I was nervous, yet anxious, excited, and cautious. As I raised the mirror, I saw this guy that looked like "Jabba the Hutt" with tubes connected and bags of blood hanging. The swelling was still very noticeable. As I slowly opened my mouth, I saw something that I could not explain. There was something foreign in my mouth and it didn't look good. I asked myself. How is this the Body of Christ?

I opened the Bible and started to read 1 Corinthians 12 again. I pondered on the words the Lord spoke to me the night before. Because of the division in the Body of Christ—the many denominations that don't want to work together, or share ideas and events, because of the fear of losing members—I would meditate on it this way.

If my tongue, not my arm-side, could speak as the Body of Christ, it would probably say. "Excuse me arm, but do you know who I am? I am his taste buds. I am his speech. You are nothing but a lowly piece of meat."

I am sure that the arm, who was placed there by God, would feel really down, depressed, and wondering what it did wrong. Isn't that what seems to be going on today in the Body of Christ. We pick people. We pick sides. We pick who we want to associate with. If they do not add anything to our lives, then we want to discard them, and not use them. We discriminately say, "They don't meet my standard."

How many times did Jesus in the Word speak about humility, unity, love, and working together?

Matthew 18:19 *Again I say unto you, that if two of you agree (in harmony, as an orchestra) on Earth as touching anything that they shall ask, it shall be done for them of my Father which is in heaven.*

You see, my arm and tongue didn't have a choice in this decision. They were placed there together to work things out.

Let me share a funny incident that happened a few months later, once I was home. One day, my daughter Deziree came to me while I was, in the kitchen, preparing my daily nutrition drink. She asked me, "Dad, are your taste buds coming back?"

She had a soda sitting on the counter. I took the can, grabbed her arm, and pulled it over the sink. She was wondering what I was about to do. I poured the soda onto her arm and said, "Well how did that taste?"

She smacked her head, with her hand, and said, "Duh!"

You see my arm does not have any attributes that my tongue had. It does not taste. When I drink something very hot it blisters. Yes, it still has hair on it that I have to shave every few weeks. It was not made to go into a mouth.

Yet, my arm and tongue are very happy together, working through the complications, and giving me something that I may have not had—Speech! You see, as people, or as the Body of Christ, we are to lift up one another, exhort one another, help one another, come along side one another, and be the one body that is in 1 Corinthians Chapter 12.

In Galatians 3:26, 27, 28 *For ye are all the children of God by faith in Christ Jesus. For as many of you as have been baptized into Christ have put on Christ. There is neither Jew nor Greek, there is neither bond or free, there is neither male nor female; for ye are all one in Christ Jesus.*

Paul clearly describes the unity of us all, explaining also in the book of Acts.

Acts 20:35 *I have showed you all things, how that labouring ye ought to support the weak, and to remember the words of the Lord Jesus, how he said, "It is more blessed to give than to receive.*

I will discuss more in Chapter 5, what the Lord has given to me to share, how that—words can make a difference.

My tongue and arm now have become one. Because of Unity, that oneness has the power to speak encouragement, bring about God's favor, and the release of many blessings. As I shared earlier, my heart will forever desire, to see the Body of Christ working together for His glory.

Matthew 5:16 *Let your light so shine before men, that they may see your good works, and glorify your Father which is in heaven.*

John 13: 34, 35 *A new commandment I give unto you, That you love one another; as I have loved you, that ye also love one another. By this shall all men know that ye are my disciples, if ye have love one to another.*

Love and Unity is a very powerful team. When two work together in Unity, with Love, God opens the windows of heaven and will pour out a blessing that cannot be contained.

CHAPTER FIVE
WORDS CAN MAKE A DIFFERENCE

Words—things that we say! Several years back, I was working at a church in Delaware with inner-city children. Each week, I had to come up with a lesson that the children could understand, by using illustrations or as we called them "object lessons." They were simply objects mostly from dollar stores or things around the house. We would use them to tell biblical stories, like Jesus telling parables throughout the Bible. One lesson was from Proverbs 18:21—

Death and Life are in the power of the tongue; and they that love it shall eat the fruit thereof."

I would call a child up front as a volunteer. In my hand would be a paper plate and a tube of toothpaste. I would tell the child on the count of three, squeeze the tube of toothpaste out as fast as you can. The children always got a kick out of this. Then I would say, 1, 2, 3 and the child would do exactly as I said. And, wow, the toothpaste would come out fast.

Conclusively, that's not the end of the lesson. I would then pull out a butter knife and ask the child to put all the toothpaste back into the tube. As you might think, the child would look at me with a puzzling stare. The rest of the children would laugh. After having the child sit down, I would go on with the lesson, explaining the power of our tongue, and that what we say, we cannot take back or get rid of it. Just like today, we have a lot of electronic devices to access major networking through, texting, internet, etc., once we send a message, you can't take it back. It's out there, and everyone can see it.

Matthew 12:36, 37 *But I say unto you, That every idle word that men shall speak, they shall give account thereof in the day of judgement. For by thy words thou shalt be justified, and by thy words thou shalt be condemned.*

For an example Jesus said in, Mark 11:23,

For verily I say unto you, That whosoever shall say unto this mountain (as lifting itself above), Be thou removed and be thou cast into the sea; and shall not doubt in his heart, but shall believe that those things which he saith shall come to pass; he shall have whatsoever he saith.

There are positive words and negative words. We can speak life, healing, encouragement, and positive ideas to others. We can also tear down someone by our tongue and words.

Proverbs 21:23 *Whosoever keepeth his mouth and his tongue keepeth his soul from troubles.*

How true, how true—how many times are we around people who love to gossip, tell stories, or just talk about themselves? Through their conversation, we feel very uncomfortable, or we start to feel weighed down or drained. Negativity will continue to be a major downfall in the Body of Christ and our individual lives. Until we get a revelation of the power of our words, we will live, defeated lives.

Remember, every time I get up in the morning or look into my mouth, I see a miracle, the Body of Christ. Again, could you imagine, if my tongue and arm started to war against each other—boy, would I be in trouble. They have learned to adapt and help one another. In James chapter 3, the brother of Jesus writes about the very same thing.

James 3:3-5, *Behold, we put bits in the horse's mouths, that they may obey us; and we turn about their whole body. Behold also the ships, which though they be so great, and are driven of fierce winds, yet are they turned about with a very small helm, whithersoever the governor listeth. Even so the tongue is a little member and boasteth great things. Behold how great a matter a little fire kindleth.*

I have had the opportunity, several times, to speak to hundreds and hundreds of people in churches, prisons, and on street corners, sharing this message about the Power of our Words. Through my journey with cancer and my tongue operation, I have been blessed to have encouraged many. I live this book each and every day. I see how people are becoming more and more negative, consuming their lives with themselves. You see, my passion is the Body of Christ, to speak to others about the importance of speaking life and death. This message has changed the way I look at people and share with people. It starts in Matthew 16: 13-26. Jesus and His disciples were traveling to the coasts of Caesarea Philippi and He asks them this question—

"Whom do men say that I the Son of man am?" They replied with "Some say you are John the Baptist, some say, Elijah the prophet, and others Jeremiah or one of the other prophets." But Jesus asked them, "But whom say ye that I am?"

Now Simon Peter heard an inner voice and spoke what he heard from that inner voice, *"Thou art the Christ, the Son of the Living God."*

Jesus replied to that statement with a word that you need to understand.

"Blessed art thou, Simon Bar-jona [his real name] for flesh and blood [man or people] hath not revealed it unto thee, but my Father which is in heaven."

Throughout our life, we encounter many people along our journey. We hear at times an inner voice—that inner voice, if you have accepted Jesus Christ as Lord and Savior, is the Holy Spirit. He is leading and guiding you in the right direction. If we are not a child of God, then that voice is the human nature, and that human nature wants nothing more but to please ourselves.

Here is the challenge in our daily walk. We have a choice to listen to the inner voice of truth (Holy Spirit) or the inner voice of our past that wants to be right. We can see this in Isaiah 14:13-15, where we see Lucifer, who became Satan (the devil), kicked out of heaven, for wanting to exalt himself above God.

For thou hast said in thine heart, I will ascend into heaven, I will exalt my throne above the stars of God; I will sit also upon the mount of the congregation, in the sides of the north; I will ascend above the heights of the clouds; I will be like the most High. Yet, thou shalt be brought down to hell, to the sides of the pit.

Peter heard that inner voice of truth and then Jesus makes a profound statement.

Vs. 18, *and I say unto thee, That thou art Peter, and upon this rock I will build my church; and the gates of hell shall not prevail against it.*

Jesus explains to Peter, because you heard that inner voice and recognized that it was from the Father in Heaven, you now will be able to discern when you hear that voice—in the future.

Again, there are two voices. The inner voice, Jesus, identified to Peter is called a "Rhema" Word—or a revelation Word from God. Have you ever been sitting in church, or listening to a preacher on television or radio, and heard something that all of a sudden made you say, "Wow! Now I understand!" What you heard is called—Rhema Word. Jesus said to Peter—upon that very Rhema Word, I will build my church.

Throughout the world, many people look at that word in Matthew and have built a CHURCH on Peter—him as an apostle. Many have built a theology around this scripture. However, if we continue on, Jesus provides us with more information about what he is saying to Peter and to us.

John 1:1-4, 14 *In the beginning was the WORD [Jesus] and the WORD, [Jesus] was with God, and the WORD [Jesus] was God. The same was in the beginning with God. All things were made by him; and without him was not anything made that was made. In him is life, and the life was the light of men. And the light shineth in darkness; and the darkness comprehended it not. And the WORD [Jesus] was made flesh, and dwelt among us, and we beheld his glory, the glory as of the only begotten of the Father full of grace and truth.*

The WORD (Jesus) asked Peter, who He (the WORD) was? The WORD (Jesus) is the living revealed word to us from God.

Vs. 19 Jesus explains to Peter the reward for hearing that inner voice called "Rhema Word" that he heard. Now think about us today. When we read the Word or the Bible, it speaks to us and changes us from within, and changes our heart. Just like that night when the Lord asked me, "What do you have in your mouth?".

When I read the Word, in 1 Corinthians 12:12-26, God started revealing to me the "Rhema Word." No one can steal that away from me. I know that I know that I know what He was revealing to me. I understood, when I read the Bible that He was using this operation and journey, for an opportunity, to minister to the Body of Christ. Jesus states in vs. 19 of Matthew chapter 16—

"And I will give thee the keys of the kingdom of heaven; and whatsoever thou shalt bind on earth shall be bound in heaven, and whatsoever thou shalt loose of earth shall be loosed in heaven."

So what is Jesus explaining here to Peter? When you hear that inner voice of truth that speaks to your heart, you now have power to SPEAK authority to the things on Earth and Heaven. Whatever we speak, we have the power to bring into our lives and others, LIFE and DEATH.

Are you getting it now?

When we listen to the things of this world and gossip, complain, backbite, and speak negative, we will eat of the fruit that we sow. But, understanding the power of the Word of God as it speaks to our heart, we can bring life to people.

But hold on, here is another lesson, as Peter listens to another voice and gets into trouble.

Jesus, in vs. 20-21, shares with his disciples that He was about to go to the cross and suffer, He would be killed, and would rise again on the third day. But, Peter heard that earthly, fleshly voice (that other voice) that wanted to think his way. Not only did he hear that voice, but he acted on that voice—by speaking. Speaking the words of that other voice is the point of damage and transferal of authority to the enemy.

In Genesis chapter 1, God uses the words—and God said. Now think about this, God did not think things into existence, God SPOKE things into existence. So, there was power in speaking words, for creation to manifest.

Back to Matthew 16:22. *Then Peter took Jesus, and began to rebuke Jesus ! "Saying, Be it far from thee, Lord; this shall NOT BE UNTO THEE."*

Death and Life are in the power of the tongue.

Peter received power, to bind and loose, on this earth, and in Heaven, because he heard an inner voice speaking to him. That voice was the voice of truth—the Holy Spirit. Conversely, when Jesus shared with the disciples about what He was about to do, Peter didn't want to hear it. He voiced his desire and told Jesus that He was not going to die. His other voice, the voice of his human nature, wanted it his way, and not God's way.

Matthew 16:23 *But he (Jesus) turned and said, Peter, Get thee behind me, Satan; thou art an offence unto me;*

for thou savourest not the things that be of God; but those that be of men.

Notice who Jesus spoke too?

He looked to Peter, but spoke at SATAN! Our human thoughts desire worldly things. The Spiritual thoughts desire Spiritual things. When we speak out worldly thoughts, we give authority over to the enemy to accomplish the things that oppose God's plan. There is "the dilemma."

It is the battle we face each and every day, when and what to speak to others. Jesus had to speak to the words that Peter had spoken, because when Peter spoke them, he did not understand that the words he spoke could have stopped Jesus from going all the way to the cross.

Jesus knew from where Peter's words came. The enemy wants to use us, to speak negative things into our life. Which if we do speak, will ultimately bring death, not only to the people to whom we speak, but to ourselves.

Words can make a difference! When the Lord revealed to me about my arm and tongue, together as one, it took me awhile to understand that my tongue is the muscle that forms the words that I speak. My tongue has the taste buds that give me that sweet and sour taste. My tongue lets me feel when liquid is hot or cold. My arm is there to assist, but whatever my tongue does, my arm goes along with it.

The times in our lives, when we are in a situation, where those around us are speaking words that offend, hurt, or bring death to others, are times just like my arm, we were going along for the ride.

Learn to listen.

God gave us two ears and one mouth. Maybe we should be listening twice as much then we speak. Psalms 107:20, *He sent his Word, and healed them, and delivered them from their destruction.*

One of the greatest lies that Satan has fed the world through little children is the adage, "Sticks and Stones may break my bones, but words will never harm me." As children, even into adulthood, we use words against one another, and all to make us feel better. But does it? So, the next time you start to speak! Think about from where that voice is coming?

Psalms 103:20 *Bless the Lord, ye his angels, that excel in strength, that do his commandments, hearkening unto the voice of his word.*

Ephesians 6:12 *For we wrestle not against flesh and blood, but against principalities, against powers, against the rulers of darkness of this world, against spiritual wickedness in high places.*

Jesus knew this battle. Peter, along with us, struggle on a daily basis. When we speak positive words, we loose God's hands to provide, protect, and bring peace. When we speak negative words, we release principalities, powers, rulers and wickedness to do the very thing we say.

CHAPTER SIX
UNITY, IT HAS POWER

Psalms 133 *"Behold how good and how pleasant it is for brethren to dwell together in UNITY! It is like the precious ointment upon the head, that ran down the beard, even Aaron's beard; that went down to the skirts of his garments; As the dew of Hermon, and the dew that descended upon the mountains of Zion; for there the Lord commanded the blessing, even life for evermore."*

The New Testament church, in the book of Acts, opens the door for us to see and understand the power of Unity and Words operating through prayer, intercession, and action. In this chapter, I will conclude and encourage you to seek and understand the journey that the Lord took me through with the battle of cancer. The Lord had been, and continues to encourage me to share this message, whenever and wherever He leads me. As a first time author, I pray that through this book of testimonies and sharing—about the tongue working together with Unity, you will not only build your life, but also those around you.

Acts 1:14 *These all continued with one accord in prayers and supplication, with the women, and Mary the mother of Jesus, and with the brethren.*

Acts 2:1 *And when the day of Pentecost was fully come, they were all in one accord in one place.*

Acts 2:46 *And they continuing daily with one accord in the temple, and breaking bread from house to house, did eat their meat with gladness and singleness of heart.*

Acts 4:24 *And when they heard that, they lifted up their voice to God with one accord, and said, Lord thou art God, which hast made heaven, and earth, and the sea, and all that in them is:*

Acts 5:12 *And by the hands of the apostles were m any signs and wonders wrought among the people; and they were all with one accord in Solomon's porch.*

Acts 8:6 *And the people with one accord gave heed unto those things which Philip spake, hearing and seeing the miracles which he did.*

Acts 12:20 *And Herod was highly displeased with them of Tyre and Sidon; but they came with one accord to him , and, having made Blastus the king's chamberlain their friend, desired peace; because their country was nourished by the king's country.*

Acts 15:25 *It seemed good to us, being assembled with one accord, to send chosen men unto you with our beloved Barnabas and Paul.*

Throughout these scriptures, the church survived and thrived on being in one accord. Over the centuries, the church has been divided into two categories. What we see today is His church and The Church. Over the years, The Church has grown in size and money, yet has lacked in unity and power. The Word of God has slowly been watered down to a tolerable or easy message to hear. The Church has become a profitable money maker even as it was during the time of Jesus.

Matthew 21:12, *And Jesus went into the temple of God, and cast out all them that sold and bought in the temple, and overthrew the tables of the moneychangers, and the seats of them that sold Doves.*

The temple was made and designed to worship the Lord God Almighty. In the Old Testament, you had to bring the appropriate sacrifice to the altar to make atonement for your sins. Jesus was still under the law before he died on the cross. Accordingly, at that time, the temple leaders allowed people to sell animals in the temple yard. It helped those who were coming from a distance not have to worry, about bringing a sacrifice with them. They could buy a sacrifice in the temple yard. Think about it, being able to come to church and use someone else's money to put into the offering plate. That would be pretty sad today.

We have many different churches today because some interpret the Bible one way and another church interprets the Bible another way. Thus, division takes hold of the church. Division to Satan is like Unity with God. I shared, in an earlier chapter, how my arm and tongue have become one, and even though they each have a separate job, they need to work together as one. As one unit (Unity) there is power and peace.

Today there are many organizations that use this power for good or evil. They have harnessed one of the keys talked about when Jesus told Peter, "I have given you the keys to the Kingdom." He would now be able to loose and bind.

45

An example: There is a law on this earth called "Gravity." Gravity exists whether you agree with it or not. If I were to go atop a ten story building and walk off. What would happen? Yes, gravity or the LAW of Gravity kicks in. I can flap my arms all I want, but I will hit the ground. So, is there a way to come against gravity? Yes, if I were to get onboard an airplane, I would by rules of the LAW of Gravity, come against that Law. As long as I am in the plane, gravity does not apply to me. But if, I were to open the door and walk out, the Law of Gravity now kicks in. One of the keys of the Kingdom is "Unity." Just like Gravity, you don't have to believe to be in it. Gravity exists. Unity exists. When two touch and agree on something on earth, there is a key that is released. Whether good or evil, this is the power that belongs to organizations that operate in Unity.

In Genesis Chapter 11, in the land of Shinar, people came to build a tower. That tower was known as the "Tower of Babel." In vs. 4 they said, *"Let us build us a city and a tower, whose top may reach unto heaven; and let us make us a name, lest we be scattered abroad upon the face of the whole earth"*.

Notice the unity. With words like—"US" we see that they had one vision, and one plan. Although it was self-centered, they had a goal. Vs. 5 it says, "And the Lord came down to see the city and the tower, which the children of men built. And the Lord said, Behold the people is one, and they have all one language; and this they begin to do; and now NOTHING will be restrained from them, which they have imagined to do."

So there you have it, the power of unity.

It is a key, and if people apply that key principle to their lives, whether good or evil, it will work just like the

Law of Gravity. As the Body of Christ, we have been faced with no unity, therefore no power. When someone in the Body of Christ suffers, we say, "Well I'll pray for you". Yes that is good, but what about coming along side and helping that person. Or, when someone says something against someone, we activate our selfishness and chime right in. Doing so, we give power to the enemy and allow him to have an advantage in our lives.

We, the Body of Christ, His church should be able to take this world on by storm, because we are His children. Unity is an action word. We have to do something. If we wait until someone else comes to us to help, we may be waiting for a long time. Our action should be a daily and moment by moment, as the Lord opens doors before us. We can plan all we want, but the greatest joy is being ready in season and out of season.

Time, and healing had passed and I was about to go through radiation therapy. My radiation doctor was Dr. Quan from Korea. He was a believer in Jesus Christ. Every week, I had to go and get a check-up during the 30 treatments I received. This one week Dr. Quan had come in just like he always did, saying, "How do you feel this week."

But this time I noticed he came in limping. I asked him, "How do you feel?"

His answer was that he hurt his foot while playing ice hockey. The first thing I said to him, "when you get done with my exam, I want to lay hands and pray for you."

He replied, "Sure, OK."

He finished his exam and started to walk out. I jumped up and said, "Dr. Quan, please take a seat. I want to pray for you." He sat down in the seat. I knelt down and laid hands on his foot believing for a miracle as I prayed. After the prayer, he thanked me. I went through the next week of radiation treatments and my regular exam that week. As I was sitting, waiting for him to come in, the door opened, and in walked a healed man. Dr. Quan jumped up and down. He laughed and thanked me for praying for him.

You see, we are the Body of Christ, by joining together in unity and speaking the Word of God we have power. When we come against one another we are defeated. A pastor told me one time, "Eric, a believer can never fail."

As I thought about that statement, he continued with, "The only time we fail, is when we talk about someone else. Because when we do, we are talking about Jesus."

That statement has always been on my mind for years. Just like that dream when I saw Jesus cutting His wrist. Life can be so much fun. People around us can be challenging. I always keep on my mind, "Do I want to be part of the problem or part of the solution?"

Psalms 133:3 *How GOOD and how PLEASANT it is for brethren to dwell together in UNITY.*

Proverbs 4:20-22 *My son, give attention to my words; incline your ear to my sayings, DO NOT let them depart from your sight. Keep them in the midst of your heart. For they are LIFE to those who find them, and HEALTH to all their whole body."*

CHAPTER SEVEN
WHAT'S NEXT?

I pray that throughout this book you have seen the hand of God move in my life, despite that it could have been a tragedy. A message I shared at the River Church, my home church, in which I pastor, was called, "A Good Cup of Coffee."

The message derived from the Old Testament story of Joseph and his brothers coupled with Jonah's encounter with the great fish. Both believed God, but Jonah didn't want to listen. He fought God the whole way and ended up on the shore of Nineveh, where God wanted him in the first place. Joseph was, thrown into a pit, left for dead, sold into slavery, jailed--in the end, before becoming the second in command of Egypt. There he was positioned to help his brothers, who threw him away in the first place.

God has a plan, and that plan will be accomplished with you or without you. God wants to do it with you. If you like a good cup of coffee, then you can appreciate this illustration. On your counter are coffee grounds. Its coffee, but it is not a good cup of coffee. Needed, is a coffee filter, but it is still not a good cup of coffee. Needed, is hot water, but that by itself will not a good cup of coffee. Sugar is great and sweet, but alone it will not make a good cup of coffee. Needed, is milk or creamer, but again, neither alone will make a good cup of coffee. Now take all of these items together, put them in a coffee maker, and from there to a cup and you will then have a "Good Cup of Coffee."

Just like our lives, we go through many different problems, situations, and troubles, whether by our own selfish ways, or the result of opposition. God has a beautiful way to turn events around for our good and ultimately bless others. Cancer is a nasty, killing disease, and maybe you know someone who has it or has had it. I want to encourage you to give that person this book. Let encouragement come to them from someone that has gone through the same or similar experience.

CHAPTER EIGHT
THE GREATEST GIFT!

The greatest gift I could ever give you or someone else is my friend Jesus. He has been there when things were dark and when things seemed hopeless. Growing up in a Lutheran Church, all my life, until I got married, gave me the roots to understand the bible. However, it wasn't until I understood that I couldn't save myself, and I needed a savior, that I truly desired more of Him. You see, I learned that a church, a religion, a pastor, a friend, or anything I do—can't save me from eternal damnation.

I grew up knowing the Bible Stories. I went through all my years of grammar and high school in church. And then one day, at an Amway Conference, on a Sunday, I heard the words of truth. "You need to accept Jesus in your heart."

From then on, I understood that a relationship with Jesus was the most important. Maybe today you want to know that peace, and joy that I have found in Him (Jesus). I would like you to read the following statements and allow the living God to speak to you by that inner voice, just like Peter.

Romans 3:23 *"For all have sinned and come short of the Glory of God."*

The first thing is to agree with God that you have done things wrong (that is called sin) like telling lies, stealing, gossip, etc.

The second thing is agree with God that I need to be born again. What is that? In John 3:1-8, Jesus is confronted with a Pharisee by the name of Nicodemus. Nicodemus reports to Jesus, *"Rabbi, we know that thou art a teacher come from God; for no man can do these miracles that thou doesn't, except God be with him."*

And Jesus responds, *"Verily, verily I say unto thee, except a man be born again, he cannot see the kingdom of God."*

Nicodemus asked, *how can a man go back into his mother's womb?*

Jesus answered, *Except a man be born of water and of the Spirit, he cannot enter into the Kingdom of God.*

In John 14:6 *Jesus saith unto him, I am the way, the truth, and the life; no man cometh unto the Father, but by me."* John 3:16 *"For God so loved the world, that he gave his only begotten son, that WHOSOEVER (that's you and me) believeth in Him should not perish, but have everlasting Life."*

The third thing is admit to God that you cannot do anything to have this relationship with Him. You can't buy it or earn it through works or giving. Ephesians 2:8 *For by grace are ye saved, through faith, and not of yourself, it is a GIFT of God.*

The fourth thing is you need to repent. Ask for forgiveness. Luke 13:3 *"except ye repent, ye shall all likewise perish. Repentance is the KEY to freedom. We hold onto things in our past, and Jesus said, "When the Son sets you free, you are free indeed."*

The fifth thing is you need to ask Jesus into your heart and life. Romans 10:13 *"For whosoever (that's you and me) shall call upon the name of the Lord shall be saved, (or born again).*

Just say to Jesus, "Come into my life. I need you. I know you died for me, rose again, and are coming back for me soon. Lord, take my life and use it for your Glory."

You are now a Child of the Living God. 2 Cor. 5:17 *"Therefore if any man be in Christ, he is a new creature, old things are passed away, behold all things are become new."*

You now have a new life in Jesus Christ.

Simple...right?

What do you do now?

Ask God to send you to a Bible teaching, Spirit-filled church that will nurture you, encourage you, come along side you, and teach you the ways of Jesus Christ. That's called "Discipleship" or being a disciple of Jesus. Share with others that you have a new life. BUT, beware, not everyone is going to be happy that you are now a Christian.

Pray, Read the Bible, and trust the Lord! I have been walking with the Lord for thirty-four years (1980), and although I am a pastor, I still have a lot to learn. So, do not be discouraged! But be encouraged, because "Greater is He that is within you, than he that is in the world."

Start to practice speaking words of encouragement, when you are strong and ready, pray for those around you. I want to thank you again, for being a part of my testimony, and teaching on Words and Unity. I pray that this book has been an eye opening experience. It has been a pleasure to write it. Your life will never be the same from this day forward, as you look into the mirror, and see the Body of Christ.

Allow me to pray for you now. *"Father in the name of your Son Jesus, I come before you and thank you for the person reading this book. As you have done the miraculous in my life, I pray that you would encourage, touch, heal, and save this reader. May your blessings be upon them and your Spirit in them. I speak healing, blessings, encouragement, joy, and Life into them right now. Go with them and guide them by your Spirit. Increase their wisdom and knowledge of your dear Son—Jesus. I pray this in Jesus Name. Amen."*

Please take this book and pass it on. Continue to pray for me and my family as we share this testimony with others. Be encouraged. One day, I hope to see you, as we walk with the one who redeemed us—Jesus Christ.

ABOUT THE AUTHOR

Eric G. Zeidler is an ordained minister and has been in full time ministry preaching the Gospel for 24 years, locally in the Delaware Valley area and around the world in Haiti, Romania, Bahamas, and the East Coast of America. He currently pastors The River Church in Penns Grove, NJ which he started 20 years ago.

He accepted Jesus Christ as his savior and Lord in 1980 at an Amway Conference in DC, and has never looked back. Eric has started many ministries over the years dealing from food distribution, to homeless outreach, to joining with other ministries to work together as the Body of Christ. CTF-TV a 24/7 radio/internet program is another way he shares the message of the Gospel around the world, while helping others who have God given talents.

Eric's passion is "the Body of Christ" working with other churches, ministries, and organizations to be the light to a hurting world.

Pastor Eric, his ministry, or The River Church can be contacted via the below information:

Pastor Eric Zeidler
PO Box 486
Swedesboro NJ 08085

www.ctf-tv.com

(Facebook) River Church

The River Church
222 South Broad St.
Penns Grove, NJ 08069
(856) 514-2206

www.therivernj.com

The Journey through Pictures

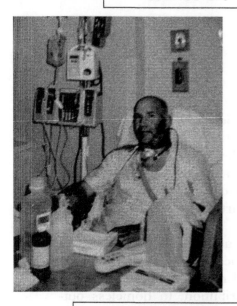 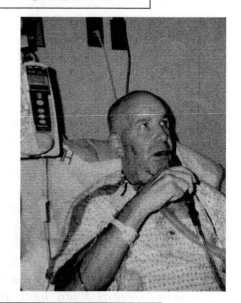

After Surgery – Recovery Begins

Before Going In – And After Losing 50lb

The Arm Unites with the Tongue

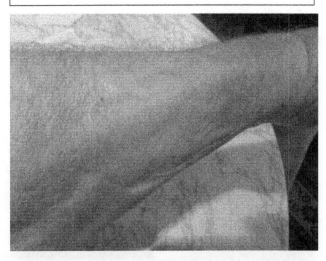

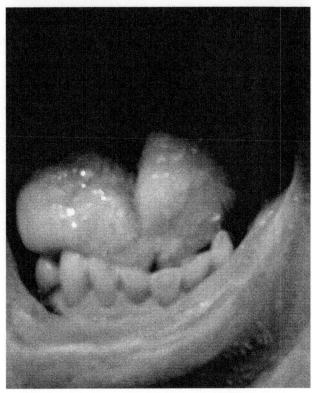

And the Two Are One
Eric & Jaimie

One at the River
The River Church
(Converted Library)

One Family
The Zeidler's Family Enjoying Life on the Ocean

This book was published by:
The Glory Cloud publications LLC
P.O. Box 193
Sicklerville, NJ 08081
www.theglorycloudpublications.com
vof1@aol.com

For additional information about us and how to obtain
other literature, or how to publish your life story,
testimony, miracle report, biography, fiction,
or children's story book, please write or email us at
the above addresses.

Psalms 68:11
*Habakkuk 2:3, 4 *2 Corinthians 1-7*
Jude 22

With our Voice and His Glory, by Faith
Making a Difference in the World

References

1. *All biblical scriptures are from the King James Version of the bible unless otherwise noted*

Books Sales and Contributions

$1.00 each of sales per book goes to these organizations

www.lifetoday.org
LIFE Outreach International
P.O. Box 982000
Fort Worth, TX 76182-8000

www.oralcancerfoundation.org
The Oral Cancer Foundation
3419 Via Lido #205
Newport Beach, CA 92663

CPSIA information can be obtained
at www.ICGtesting.com
Printed in the USA
BVOW11s1125120817
491556BV00004B/28/P